# The REDWALL Cookbook

# The REDWALL Cookbook

## BRIAN JACQUES

ILLUSTRATED BY

CHRISTOPHER DENISE

PHILOMEL BOOKS

# TABLE OF CONTENTS

## Spring

Hare's Pawspring Vegetable Soup ............................................... 5

Crispy Cheese'n'Onion Hogbake .............................................. 7

Vegetable Casserole à la Foremole ............................................ 9

Gourmet Garrison Grilled Leeks ............................................. 11

Stuffed Springtide Mushrooms ............................................... 13

Abbot's Special Abbey Trifle ................................................. 15

Custard Sauce ................................................................. 15

Spiced Gatehouse Tea Bread .................................................. 17

Honeybaked Apples ........................................................... 19

Hot Mint Tea ................................................................. 21

## Summer

Hotroot Sunsalad ............................................................. 31

Brockhall Badger Carrot Cakes ............................................... 32

Great Hall Gooseberry Fool .................................................. 33

Cheerful Churchmouse Cherry Crisp .......................................... 35

Rosey's Jolly Raspberry Jelly Rock Cakes .................................... 37

Afternoon Tea Scones with Strawberry Jam and Cream ....................... 39

Squirrelmum's Blackberry and Apple Cake ................................... 41

Guosim Shrew Shortbread .................................................... 42

Summer Strawberry Fizz ...................................................... 45

# Autumn

Mole's Favourite Deeper'n'Ever Turnip'n'Tater'n'Beetroot Pie — 53

Bellringer's Reward (Roast Roots and Baked Spuds) — 55

October Ale — 57

Autumn Oat Favourites — 60

Hare's Haversack Crumble — 61

Harvestberry Sunset Pudd — 63

Loamhedge Legacy Nutbread — 63

Dibbun's Delight — 66

Golden Hill Pears — 67

# Winter

Shrimp'n'Hotroot Soup — 73

Veggible Molebake — 75

Stones inna Swamp — 78

Savoury Squirrel Bakes — 81

Outside'n'Inside Cobbler Riddle — 84

Rubbadeedubb Pudd — 86

Nunnymolers — 87

Applesnow — 88

Mossflower Mulled Cider — 89

*For Constance, who collected the recipes—B.J.*

*For Anika, Sofia, and Isabel—C.D.*

PHILOMEL BOOKS

A division of Penguin Young Readers Group

Published by The Penguin Group

Penguin Group (USA) Inc., 375 Hudson Street, New York, NY 10014, U.S.A.

Penguin Group (Canada), 10 Alcorn Avenue, Toronto, Ontario, Canada M4V 3B2

(a division of Pearson Penguin Canada Inc.)

Penguin Books Ltd, 80 Strand, London WC2R 0RL, England.

Penguin Ireland, 25 St. Stephen's Green, Dublin 2, Ireland

(a division of Penguin Books Ltd.)

Penguin Group (Australia), 250 Camberwell Road, Camberwell, Victoria 3124, Australia

(a division of Pearson Australia Group Pty Ltd).

Penguin Books India Pvt Ltd, 11 Community Centre, Panchsheel Park, New Delhi - 110 017, India.

Penguin Group (NZ), Cnr Airborne and Rosedale Roads, Albany, Auckland 1310, New Zealand

(a division of Pearson New Zealand Ltd).

Penguin Books (South Africa) (Pty) Ltd, 24 Sturdee Avenue, Rosebank, Johannesburg 2196, South Africa.

Penguin Books Ltd, Registered Offices: 80 Strand, London WC2R 0RL, England.

Published simultaneously in Canada.  Manufactured in China by South China Printing Co. Ltd.

Design by Semadar Megged and Marikka Tamura. Text set in Perpetua.

The artwork was created with acrylic paint and charcoal.

Library of Congress Cataloging-in-Publication Data

Jacques, Brian.

The Redwall cookbook / Brian Jacques ; illustrated by Christopher Denise.   p. cm.

Includes index. 1. Cookery—Juvenile literature. 2. Food in literature. I. Denise, Christopher. II. Title.

TX652.5.J36 2005    641.5—dc22    2005003470    ISBN 0-399-23791-7

1 3 5 7 9 10 8 6 4 2

First Impression

When I was a young fellow, food was short because of World War II. Everything was on ration, and lots of things folk liked were just unobtainable. So, there I was, reading through my mother's old cookery books, my mouth watering at the coloured illustrations of delicious recipes. And the books I'd read in the library. . . It really annoyed me when I'd come to a passage where somebody ate a marvellous feast. There never seemed to be any description of it. Afterward, the hero would ride off on his white stallion, thanking the King for the wonderful dinner. *Wait!* What did it taste like? What did it look like? How was it made? Did he really enjoy it? Questions that even to my young mind required much answering. That is why the fare at Redwall Abbey is featured so prominently—I'm trying to put things right! In my stories, the food has as much a part of the saga as the battle, the quest, the poems, the riddles, and the songs. So enjoy it, mates! But in moderation—don't try to be a gluttonous hare. Also, make sure you have proper supervision in the handling of knives, hot stoves, and things like that. I hope you enjoy the recipes. They all work, you know. Wot wot!

*Brian Jacques*

𝕎hen deciding on a recipe,
keep in mind the following legend:

Adult supervision required

Child/Dibbun friendly

**A**TTENTION! Hearken and pay heed!
This is something you must read.
The Kitchen Rules of old Redwall
for Dibbuns an' young 'uns—in fact, for all!

Do not play around stoves and hot ovens. (Burnt tails!)
Do not mess with sharp knives. (Cut paws!)
Always ask Mum first, or Dad. (Some dads are good cooks, too!)
Do not try to lift off hot pots or pans or lids by yourself and
do not try to reach high shelves or cupboards.
Ask a big 'un to do these things for you.
They'll always help if you mind your manners and ask politely.
(Try it and see!)
If you have little brothers and sisters helping you, take care.
Keep an eye on them and see they don't get harmed.
(Or they won't grow up to be big and sensible like you!)
When you are finished cooking, clean up after yourself.
(All the best cooks do—Nanna will tell you that!)
Last of all, happy cooking (and tasty eating)!

*Skipper of Otters*

# Spring

Here's a secret you don't know,
'twas just a day or two ago
when rain washed winter's snow away.
I heard two mousewives say,
I think the spring will soon be here,
oh my word, oh joy, oh dear!
The ice upon the pond is gone,
and see that bird, the chirpy one?
I tell you, 'tis no jest,
she's built herself a nest.
Oh well, I never, gracious me!
Pray, what else do you see?
Why, bluebells, crocus, daffodils,
sprouting up 'twixt vale and hills,
and grass upon the lea I've seen,
like gentle mist of green.
'Tis not like me to gossip, dear,
but this is what I hear—
Out in the woods, I tell you true,
I've heard the first cuckoo!
*Cuckoo* he cried, now spring is born,
look forward to each shining morn.
So hurry, ladies—haste indoors,
for your spring cleaning chores!

3

Friar Hugo bustled his way around the Redwall Abbey kitchens. He was a very busy mouse. A cook's hat wobbled on his head as he mopped at his brow with the dock leaf attached to his tail. Hugo's tubby form appeared and disappeared between ovens and ranges of steaming pans, squeaking out orders to his assistants. There was only one way to do things in the Abbey kitchen—Friar Hugo's way.

"Durdlum, scrub that chopping board clean. Sister Pansy, fetch the spring vegetables. There's peeling and chopping to be done, lots of it!"

Sister Pansy was the prettiest young mouse. She loved cooking and had been around the kitchens since she could first toddle. Pushing a laden trolley of vegetables to the chopping block, Pansy chatted away as she unloaded them. "Most of these have been picked fresh this morning. Oh, isn't it exciting, Friar? The Springtide Sunfeast!"

Friar Hugo helped Pansy with the vegetables. He liked the young mouse; she was intelligent and hard-working. "Springtime was made for good young 'uns like you, Pansy. Tell you what—I'll teach you how to prepare a Springtide Sunfeast. How would you like that, little Sister?"

Pansy's eyes went wide with delight.

"Oh, I'd love that, Friar! Thank you. Just tell me what you need, and I'll try my best to help. What's first?"

Hugo scanned the menu. "Hare's Pawspring Vegetable Soup. It's an old recipe from Basil Stag Hare's family. They say it improves their pawspringing powers. It think it must—have you ever seen a hare leaping about at springtime? Remarkable! Now, here's how it's made. Pay attention."

4

# Hare's Pawspring Vegetable Soup

*Serves 4*

## Ingredients:

1 tablespoon unsalted butter

3 medium carrots, peeled and sliced

2 medium onions, peeled and chopped

2 celery stalks, chopped

¼ cup tomato paste

2 vegetable bouillon cubes, crumbled

Salt and pepper, to taste

2 cups (4 ounces) shredded green
  cabbage

½ cup (2 ounces) sliced green beans

1 teaspoon cornstarch

Crusty bread, for serving

## Method:

1. Melt the butter in a large saucepan over medium heat. Add the carrots, onions and celery and cook, stirring, for 4 minutes (do not let the vegetables brown).

2. Stir in the tomato paste and bouillon cubes, add 4 ½ cups water, and season with salt and pepper.

3. Bring to a boil, stirring, then cover the pan, reduce the heat, and simmer for 10 minutes.

4. Stir in the cabbage and green beans, cover again, and simmer until the vegetables are tender, another 10 minutes.

5. In a bowl, blend the cornstarch with a little warm water and stir it into the soup. Bring the soup back to a boil, stirring continuously, and cook for 2 minutes.

6. Reduce the heat and simmer, uncovered, for 10 more minutes, then add salt and pepper if needed and serve the soup with crusty bread.

$\mathcal{A}$mbrose Spike, Redwall's Cellar Keeper, rolled a barrel of his famous October Ale into the kitchens. The sturdy old hedgehog mopped his brow with a spotted kerchief.

"There ye are, Friar—October Ale brewed by me own paw last autumn season. I 'opes yore makin' some Crispy Cheese'n'Onion Hogbake. I likes a chunk when it goes cold. 'Tis very tasty for lunch when I'm busy in my cellar. Now then, young Pansy, I 'ope yore peelin' those veggibles proper. Always peel away from yoreself, an' keep the other paw behind the knife. That's the way! Friar, can I stay an' watch you makin' the Hogbake?"

Hugo patted the Cellarhog's spikes carefully. "Of course you can, Ambrose. Then you can learn how to make it for yourself. It's quite simple, really."

# Crispy Cheese'n'Onion Hogbake

*Serves 4*

## Method:

1. Preheat the oven to 350° F.

2. Place the onions in the bottom of a large casserole dish. Sprinkle the cheese over the onions; pour in the beaten egg and milk and season with salt and pepper.

3. Sprinkle the cornflakes over all and arrange the slices of tomato to cover.

4. Bake in the centre of the oven for 40 minutes. Serve hot.

## Ingredients:

2 medium onions, chopped

2 cups (4 ounces) grated Cheddar cheese

4 eggs, beaten

¾ cup milk

Salt and pepper, to taste

1 ½ cups cornflakes, crushed

4 tomatoes, sliced

Foremole trundled in with the next trolley of vegetables. He tugged his snout politely to Hugo and Pansy. The mole's quaint accent made Pansy smile.

"Oi've cummed to make 'ee moi special cassyroller, zurr!"

Hugo bowed graciously to the mole Chieftain. "I was hoping you would, my friend. Whew, it's hot in here. Are you coming for a breath of fresh air out on the lawn, Pansy?"

However, the young Sister had other ideas. "You go, Friar. I wouldn't want to miss Foremole making his cassyroller. I wonder what it is exactly?"

Hugo chuckled. "We call it Vegetable Casserole à la Foremole. By all means, Pansy, stay and watch, but write the recipe down. I'd like to hear how our friend makes it."

Foremole grinned from ear to ear. "Bo urr, an' so 'ee shall, zurr, an' 'ee too, likkle Sister."

# Vegetable Casserole à la Foremole

## Ingredients:

Unsalted butter, for the casserole dish

4 large potatoes, scrubbed and sliced

4 medium carrots, peeled and sliced

1 turnip or $1/2$ a rutabaga, peeled and diced

4 leeks, cleaned and sliced

1 cup vegetable stock

Salt and pepper, to taste

$3/4$ cup breadcrumbs, preferably whole wheat

2 cups (4 ounces) grated sharp Cheddar cheese

## Method:

1. Preheat the oven to 350° F. Grease a large casserole dish with butter.

2. Arrange the vegetables in alternate layers in the dish, beginning and ending with potatoes.

3. Pour the stock over the vegetables and season with salt and pepper.

4. Cover with a lid or foil and bake for 1 $1/2$ hours.

5. In a bowl, mix together the breadcrumbs and cheese and sprinkle them on top of the casserole.

6. Return the dish to the oven and bake, uncovered, until the topping is crisp and starting to brown, 10 to 15 more minutes.

riar Hugo did not stay out on the lawn for long. No sooner had Foremole departed than Hugo came scuttling back in. "Look out, Pansy. Basil and his nephew are coming—we're under siege from the famine family!"

Pansy could not help giggling as the two hares strolled in, ears flapping and noses twitching furiously at the delicious aromas. Basil Stag Hare's nephew, Tummscoff Stag Vittlesmythe (with a *y* and not an *i*), was a young hare from a distant family branch, paying his first visit to Redwall. He had a roguish smile and an insatiable appetite, even for a hare. Foremole's casserole drew him to it like a magnet.

"What ho, I say, Nunky Baz, take a sniff of this. Jolly good rations, I'll be bound, wot wot!"

Basil tweaked the ear of his voracious nephew smartly. "Flamin' young rip, it's sah t'you. Call me Nunky Baz one more time an' I'll fricassee your confounded whiskers. Now then, Hugo, me old tatercake, have y'got the jolly old leeks?"

The Friar wagged his ladle warningly under Basil's nose. "I'm not your old tatercake, and they're not jolly old leeks. They're perfectly good new spring leeks, picked at dawn today!"

Basil inspected the leeks and chuckled. "Hawhawhaw, so they are! Just look at these, young Tummscoff—just the ticket. Hope you've got my recipe, Friar?"

Tummscoff interrupted his uncle. "Nunky Baz says that he got it from his old regimental cook. Gourmet Garrison Grilled Leeks. Never tasted 'em m'self, but they sound super duper, wot!"

Friar Hugo sighed wearily. "I was just about to start cooking them. Tummscoff, keep your thieving paws where I can see them, and you too, Nunky Baz. Behave and I'll let you watch."

Basil sniffed indignantly. "Nunky Baz, indeed! Carry on, sah!"

# GOURMET GARRISON GRILLED LEEKS

## METHOD:

1. Preheat the broiler. Bring a large pot of water to a boil and add salt. Boil the leeks for 10 minutes.

2. Drain the leeks and transfer them to a shallow ovenproof dish.

3. In a bowl, cream the butter, then beat in the cheese and mustard. Spread this mixture over the leeks.

4. Place the leeks under the broiler until golden (watch carefully so they do not burn), about 3 minutes.

*Serves 4*

## INGREDIENTS:

Salt

1 ½ pounds (about 4 medium) leeks, cleaned and chopped into 1 ½-inch lengths

2 tablespoons unsalted butter, softened

1 tablespoon grated Parmesan cheese

2 teaspoons Dijon mustard

The Father Abbot of Redwall ambled into the kitchens just in time to see Pansy chasing both hares out with a rolling pin.

"Out, out, the pair of you! That honey is for the feast, not for gluttons to dip their paws in. Out, I say!"

Tummscoff saluted the Abbot as he nipped smartly through the doorway. "Good day to you, Father. Fierce young gel, ain't she?"

The kindly old mouse winked broadly at Pansy. "Well done, Sister, but next time try a ladle. You need something lighter to chase hares from the kitchen. Well, now, I hope you've remembered my favourite dish."

Pansy curtsied prettily. "Of course, Father Abbot. I know how you like Stuffed Springtide Mushrooms. I'm going to cook them specially for you."

The Abbot beamed with pleasure. "Thank you so much, Sister Pansy. Good day, Hugo. May I ask what the dessert will be for our Springtide Sunfeast? Something marvellous, I'll wager."

Hugo wiped his brow with the dock leaf by wagging his tail. "All your favourites, Father—Honeybaked Apples, Spiced Gatehouse Tea Bread, and Abbot's Special Abbey Trifle. With lots of Hot Mint Tea to settle your digestion."

Sitting down on a vegetable trolley, the Abbot closed his eyes dreamily at the thought of it all. "My good kitchen friends, you really do spoil an old mouse!"

Pansy smiled. "Come and watch us making your mushrooms, Father."

# STUFFED SPRINGTIDE MUSHROOMS

## INGREDIENTS:

1 teaspoon vegetable oil, for the
   baking sheet
8 portobello mushrooms, wiped clean
¼ cup (½ stick) unsalted butter
1 cup breadcrumbs, preferably
   whole wheat
8 teaspoons sesame seeds
Pinch each dried parsley and dried
   thyme
Salt and pepper, to taste
1 cup (2 ounces) grated hard cheese
   (use your favourite)

## METHOD:

1. Preheat the oven to 400° F and brush a rimmed
   baking sheet with the oil.

2. Pull the stems from the mushroom caps and put the
   caps to one side. Trim away the bottoms of the stems,
   then chop the stems finely.

3. Melt the butter in a pan over medium heat and add
   the chopped mushroom stems. Cook, stirring, until
   soft, 4 to 5 minutes. Take the pan off the heat.

4. Stir the breadcrumbs, sesame seeds and herbs into the pan and season with salt
   and pepper.

5. Place the mushroom caps in the baking dish (stem side up) and spoon the filling
   into them. Sprinkle each mushroom with grated cheese.

6. Bake until the stuffing is golden brown and the cap is tender, 15 to 20 minutes.

As he laid the mushrooms on a large, flat earthenware platter, Friar Hugo winced at a chance remark from Pansy.

"Oh, look! Here's little Bungo and his Dibbun friends come to visit us."

Hugo muttered forlornly, "I thought things were going too smoothly since we got rid of Basil and young Tummscoff. Now we're under attack from that rascal Bungo and his Dibbun crew!"

The Friar waved his ladle at them. "Be off with you! A kitchen's not the place for babes. You'll end up causing an accident and getting your tails roasted. Go and play outside!"

The big, brawny form of Skipper appeared in the doorway. "Ahoy there, Friar. I'll take care o' those villains!" The otter Chieftain cleared off a low shelf and sat the Dibbuns upon it.

Bungo glared fiercely at Friar Hugo. "Us'n's wanna see ee h'Abbot's Speshul h'Abbey Troifle be gettin' made. Uz b'aint moven 'til ee make et, zurr!"

Pansy felt sorry for the molebabe and his pals. She found a bag of candied chestnuts and gave them one each.

"Now, sit still there and be good. We'll let you watch."

Skipper accepted a candied chestnut and sat with them. "Thankee, marm. We'll be good, I promise!"

The Dibbuns roared laughing at the big otter acting as if he were one of them. Friar Hugo threw up his paws.

"Ah, well. I wasn't going to make the trifle until last, but that can change. Come on, Pansy. Lend a paw here, and we'll do it together."

# Abbot's Special Abbey Trifle

## Method:

1. Place the sponge cake or ladyfinger pieces in a glass bowl.

2. In a saucepan over medium heat, combine 3 cups of the raspberries with the sugar. Cook, stirring, until the sugar has dissolved, about 2 minutes. Let cool.

3. Toss the cooked raspberries and their juices with the cake, then smooth the mixture down.

4. Pour custard sauce or pudding over the mixture, cover with plastic and leave the trifle to set in the fridge for about 2 hours.

5. Scatter another cup of raspberries on the set custard. Put the whipped cream over the raspberries in blobs and then smooth it to cover completely.

6. Decorate the top of the trifle with the toasted almonds and the remaining cup of raspberries and serve.

*Note:* ## Custard Sauce

1. In a bowl, beat the eggs and egg yolks with the sugar.

2. In a pan over medium heat, warm the milk with the vanilla bean pod and pulp (if using).

3. When the milk is steaming (do not let it boil), pour it slowly over the egg mixture, whisking constantly. Return the liquid to the pan.

4. Stirring constantly, cook over low heat until the sauce begins to thicken, about 4 minutes. Transfer immediately to a bowl. Remove the vanilla pod if necessary, or stir in the vanilla extract. Let cool. This sauce can be stored in a covered container in the refrigerator for up to 3 days.

*Note:* ## Toasting Nuts

Preheat the oven to 350° F. Spread the nuts on a rimmed baking sheet and toast, stirring halfway through, until fragrant and browned, about 5 minutes for sliced almonds. Transfer to a plate to cool.

*Serves 6 to 8*

## Ingredients:

6 cups cubed sponge cake, or 18 ladyfingers, broken into pieces

5 cups fresh or frozen raspberries

¼ cup sugar

2 ½ cups prepared or homemade custard sauce (see Note), or vanilla pudding (made from one 2 ¾ ounce package pudding mix), cooled to room temperature

1 cup heavy cream, whipped

2 tablespoons sliced almonds, toasted (see Note)

*Makes about 2 ½ cups*

## Custard Sauce

2 eggs

4 egg yolks

¼ cup sugar

2 cups milk

1 vanilla bean, pod split lengthwise, pulp scraped (or use 1 teaspoon vanilla extract)

The Dibbuns gazed in awe at the splendid trifle. Friar Hugo sighed with satisfaction. "There! Now be off with you, Dibbuns! Go and play outdoors."

The Father Abbot joined them. Sitting on the shelf next to Bungo, he tucked both paws into his habit sleeves. "Sorry. We're staying to see you make Spiced Gatehouse Tea Bread. More candied chestnuts, please, Sister Pansy!"

Bungo almost fell off the shelf with laughing. "Hurrhurrhurr! You'm got to do wot ee h'Abbot sez, zurr. Yurr, Skipper, be you a-stayen, too?"

Skipper held out his tattooed paw for a nut. "I certainly am, matey. Ain't budgin' 'til dessert's all made!"

Pansy hid a smile as she scolded Skipper and the Abbot. "You two are supposed to be showing an example. Worse than all the Dibbuns put together, you are."

The Father Abbot wrinkled his nose at her. "If we don't watch, we'll never learn anything. Right, Bungo?"

The molebabe nodded solemnly. "Roight ee are, zurr. Coom on, ee cooks. Get on wi' et, gurt lazy lumpers!"

# SPICED GATEHOUSE TEA BREAD

## METHOD:

1. Preheat the oven to 375° F and butter an 8-cup, preferably nonstick loaf pan.

2. Place the dried fruit in a large bowl. Pour the hot tea over the fruit, stir in the brown sugar and let the mixture cool for 5 minutes.

3. In a bowl, whisk together the flours, pumpkin pie spice, baking powder and salt. Stir the dry ingredients into the fruit mixture, then stir in the egg until well combined.

4. Scrape the batter into the pan, level the surface, and place in the top third of the oven. Bake until a toothpick inserted into the center of the loaf comes out clean, about 1 hour.

5. Let the loaf cool in the pan for 10 minutes, then turn it out onto a wire rack to cool completely. Slice thinly to serve.

*Makes 1 loaf*

## INGREDIENTS:

Butter, for the pan

3 cups mixed dried fruit (preferably 1 cup each raisins, currants and golden raisins)

1 $\frac{1}{2}$ cups hot brewed tea

4 packed teaspoons dark brown sugar

1 $\frac{1}{2}$ cups whole wheat flour

1 $\frac{1}{4}$ cups all-purpose flour

2 tablespoons pumpkin pie spice (or 2 teaspoons each cinnamon, ginger and nutmeg)

2 teaspoons baking powder

1 teaspoon salt

1 egg, beaten

ℳatthias, the Warrior Mouse of Redwall, was next to stride into the kitchen. He sniffed the air.

"Somebeast told me you were baking Spiced Gatehouse Tea Bread. What a delicious smell!"

His wife, the good Lady Cornflower, popped her head around the doorway. "Matthias, there you are. Hello, everyone. What are you all doing in here, may I ask?"

Friar Hugo passed his ladle to Cornflower.

"They've all come to watch you making Honeybaked Apples. There's nobeast can make 'em like you do, marm. Come on, Pansy. It's our turn to take a break!"

Everybeast had to squinch up to make room as Hugo and Pansy passed the candied chestnuts around and seated themselves on the shelf.

Matthias nodded proudly to his pretty wife. "Go on, Cornflower. Show them how it's done!"

# HONEYBAKED APPLES

## METHOD:

1. Preheat the oven to 350° F. Generously butter a baking dish.

2. Core the apples, stopping $\frac{1}{2}$ inch short of the base of the apple. Leave the peels on. Stand the apples in the buttered dish.

3. Fill each apple with 2 tablespoons of the dried fruit.

4. Pour a tablespoon of warm honey into each cavity, letting it run over a little onto the tops of the apples.

5. Pour water into the pan until it comes about $\frac{1}{2}$ inch up the sides of the apples.

6. Cover the pan with foil and bake in the bottom third of the oven for 25 to 30 minutes.

7. Serve warm with custard sauce or a drizzle of heavy cream.

*Serves 4*

## INGREDIENTS:

Butter, for the baking dish

4 medium baking apples (such as Granny Smith, McIntosh or Rome)

$\frac{1}{2}$ cup mixed dried fruit (such as raisins, currants and golden raisins)

$\frac{1}{4}$ cup honey, warmed until runny

Custard sauce (see Note, page 15) or heavy cream, for serving oisy Sam the squirrel arrived in time to see the last of the Honey-baked Apples being taken from the oven. Sam could never speak without shouting—he made everybeast jump.

"Honeybaked Apples! Why didn't somebeast tell me Lady Cornflower was makin' 'em, eh? They look wonderful!"

Basil and Tummscoff sidled in. Basil coughed politely. "Er, ahem! If y'think they look good, wait'll you taste 'em, Sam. But what are you doin' in here, old scout, wot?"

Noisy Sam roared at the hare. "What am I doin' in here? Makin' Hot Mint Tea, of course! Nobeast in the Abbey can make Hot Mint Tea like I do!"

There were murmurs of agreement from all the Redwallers. Lady Cornflower sat on the shelf, next to Matthias. "Can I watch please, Sam? I want to see how you make it so well."

Sam bowed gallantly and roared through the steam from the pans, "Be my guest, marm, an' the rest of ye, too!"

Basil and Tummscoff made a beeline for the shelf.

"I say, budge up, you bounders. Plenty o' room for two slim, handsome hares up there, wot!"

"Can I sit next to you, Nunky Baz? Don't hog those candied chestnuts, Skipper. Pass 'em along—we're famished!"

Skipper passed the nuts. "Huh, never knew a hare that wasn't."

Noisy Sam roared at them again. "Can I have a bit of quiet there? This is a very delicate operation. Right, here's how you make real Hot Mint Tea."

# Hot Mint Tea

## Method:

1. Put the tea and chopped mint leaves in a jug or teapot. Bring 5 cups of water to a boil and pour it over the tea.

2. Leave to steep for 5 minutes.

3. Strain into four big mugs and serve with honey added to taste.

*Serves 4*

## Ingredients:

2 teaspoons black tea (or 1 tea bag)

1 small bunch fresh mint, chopped

Honey, to taste

Sam received a round of applause from his audience perched upon the shelf. They declared that they had never seen Hot Mint Tea made better. Friar Hugo started counting off the dishes on his paws, continually objecting to Pansy, who kept trying to interrupt him.

"I think everything's taken care of for our Springtide Sunfeast. Let me see. There's Hare's Pawspring Vegetable Soup—"

Pansy cut in. "But Friar, do you think—"

Hugo waved his tail. "Hush, Pansy! There's Crispy Cheese 'n' Onion Hogbake—"

Pansy tugged at his apron. "Friar Hugo, I think you should listen—"

He shrugged her off. "Silence, Sister! Vegetable Casserole à la Foremole, Gourmet Garrison Grilled Leeks—"

Sam roared at Hugo. "I think ye should listen to Pansy!"

Friar Hugo frowned severely at him. "Stuffed Springtide Mushrooms—"

*Crack!!!* The shelf broke!

Everybeast fell in a heap, but luckily, some old sacks beneath the shelf broke their fall. Hugo extricated himself from beneath Bungo and a crowd of chortling Dibbuns.

"Why didn't somebeast tell me the shelf was about to break?"

Pansy managed to unwind Skipper's tail from around her neck. "I was trying to tell you, but you weren't listening!"

Groaning aloud, Basil allowed his nephew to help him up. "Me blinkin' back's broken! It'll need lots o' those leeks to straighten it up again. What d'you say, young feller, wot?"

Tummscoff lowered his uncle back onto the empty sacks.

"Oh, bad luck, Nunky Baz. You lie there an' rest your old bones. We're goin' to get washed up an' put our feastin' togs on!"

The Redwallers fled, laughing, with Basil hobbling behind.

"Bounders! Cads! I say, there—wait for a wounded Warrior, wot!"

# SUMMER

Rise, O lark, soar up on high,
sing your praises to the sky.
Come, you little humble bee,
kiss each blushing rose for me.
Fruits upon the orchard bough,
ripen sweet for summer now!

Summer steals in through my dreams,
voyaging through dawning,
like a leaf down shaded streams,
to the golden-clad morning.
Hearken to each wondrous day,
where the sun is King,
keeping warmdark night at bay,
late into soft evening.

Yonder come the hazy days,
basking in the warm sunrays.
Gently down the path 'twill soon
shimmer in the distant noon.
All the earth and we as well,
are under summer's magic spell!

A large green-and-black-banded dragonfly skimmed the surface of Redwall Abbey pond, causing tiny sun-sparkled ripples to spread. Friar Hugo fidgeted anxiously as he sat in the bankshade beneath a willow tree. Basil Stag Hare and his nephew, Tummscoff, accompanied by Foremole, sat with the Friar. Grunting contentedly, the mole leader lay back, gazing up into the cloudless blue sky. He patted Hugo's paw.

"Thurr, thurr, gudd zurr. You'm set yrr an' take ee rest naow."

Hugo's fidgeting increased. "But I don't need a rest. What in the name of seasons are Constance and Sister Pansy up to in my kitchens?" He made to rise, but Basil firmly sat him down again.

"They're in charge of makin' our Summer Orchard Picnic Tea, old lad. No need to fuss y'self, sah. Enjoy your day off—you deserve it. Tut tut, I wish you'd stop fidgetin' an wrigglin' about like a frog on a bally feather. Y'makin' me nervous, wot!"

Hugo gnawed at a pawnail; Tummscoff slapped his paw lightly. "Mustn't do that, Friar, or you'll end up eatin' your blinkin' paw. That's what Nunky Baz always says t'me."

Basil fixed his nephew with a frosty glare. "Call me Nunky Baz once more an' I'll eat your blinkin' paws off, laddie buck. Oh, stop worryin', Hugo. The picnic tea will be top-hole. Think of all those lovely ladies cookin' away, just so you can have the day off, ungrateful old bodger!"

Hugo stared unhappily at the calm, sunlit pond. "It's not that I'm un-grateful, but they're in my kitchens, using my cooking stuff. Taking things out of cupboards, putting them back in different places. I'll never be able to find anything again. It'll upset my routine!"

Foremole tried to calm the agitated cook. "Ho no, zurr, yung Sister Pansy, she be's a-knowen whurr everythin' goes. You'm take moi wurd, she'm a guddbeast."

Friar Hugo nodded agreement, then found something else to worry about.

"But I've always made the Summer Orchard Picnic Tea. Suppose they make a mess of it?"

Basil shook his head pityingly at the Friar. "Make a what . . . a mess? My dear sah, you'd better not let Constance, or Lady Cornflower, or Sister Pansy, or any of the ladies hear you makin' remarks like that. Listen t'me, old chap, I think you'll be jolly well surprised at how nice it all turns out. Right, chaps?"

His friends nodded firmly. "Right!"

Hugo muttered under his breath, "Huh, making all those recipes different to my way. Well, it had better turn out nice, because I'm going to taste everything and check how each dish was made, so there!"

In the orchard, Log-a-Log, the Guosim shrew Chief, had his shrews laying the tables. Skipper stood at the orchard entrance, fending off Dibbuns. "Away with ye, mateys. Tea ain't ready yet. Great seasons! Is that a liddle ghost I see?"

Bungo whipped the tablecloth from off his head and growled. "Hurr hurr, froikened ee, diddent oi, zurr? You'm best let oi coom in, or oi'll make 'orrible noises. *Whurrrrrr!*"

Skipper scooped up the molebabe and inspected him. "Constance Badgermum'll make 'orrible noises if'n she sees yore mucky face an' muddy paws. You an' yore Dibbuns run down to the pond now an' get scrubbed up, or you'll be gettin' early bed an' no Summer Orchard Picnic Tea!"

Whooping and squealing, the Dibbuns fled off to the pond.

Constance, Redwall's great Badgermum, trolled wearily into the orchard. She sat down and fanned her face with an apron hem.

"Phew! It's hot in those kitchens. Friar Hugo really does deserve a day off now and then. Oh, isn't everything just perfect? The tables look absolutely stunning!"

Log-a-Log bowed modestly. "Used all the best white linen, marm—best crockery an' cutlery, too. Me an' Skipper chose the flowers. 'Ope you like 'em?"

Constance wandered around the four tables set in a square. She sniffed the blossoms of sainfoin, milk vetch, forget-me-not, pasqueflower, evening primrose and charlock, letting her paws caress the fern, ivy and pimpernel, which trailed gracefully over the snowy white linen.

"They're gorgeous! Thank you all. This is the perfect setting for a real Redwall Summer Orchard Picnic Tea. I'll get my friends from the kitchen to lay out the food. Would you and Skipper like to go and tell Friar Hugo that tea is served? Take your time—walk him nice and slow."

Sunlight and shade dappled the orchard. Happy creatures laughed and gossiped as they took their places at the beautiful picnic tea. The Father Abbot sat Hugo in the seat of honour, then recited grace.

"We thank the summer season
for these bright happy days.
The memory of this wondrous noon
will stay with us always.
We thank our friends for being friends,
who came here with good heart,
and sit here patient, 'til I say,
'Friends, let the feasting start!' "

Everybeast began passing dishes around the tables, but Friar Hugo folded his paws and sat tight-lipped, even though he secretly had to admit the food looked excellent.

A cheery ottermaid named Streamwag served Hugo from a big elm burr bowl. "Come on, sir, try some o' my Hotroot Sunsalad. 'Tis made from my old Granny Sprayrudder's recipes. You'll like it."

Grudgingly, the Friar sampled the dish. He munched away thoughtfully, nodding his head and looking critical. "Hmm, your old granny certainly knew how to make Hotroot Sunsalad. Though I wouldn't have made it so hot tasting. Well, young Streamwag, tell me the recipe, please."

# Hotroot Sunsalad

*Serves 4*

## Ingredients:

### Salad:

Salt

3 medium parsnips, peeled and cut
   into matchsticks

3 medium carrots, peeled and cut into
   matchsticks

4 medium Jerusalem artichokes,
   peeled and thinly sliced

1 leek, cleaned and thinly sliced

### Dressing:

¼ cup wine vinegar

2 tablespoons extra-virgin olive oil

Dash of hot pepper sauce

Pinch of salt

## Method:

1. To make the salad, bring a large pot of salted water to a boil. Plunge the vegetables into the water and boil until cooked but still crisp, 6 to 8 minutes. Drain the vegetables and transfer them to a serving bowl.

2. While the vegetables are cooking, place all the dressing ingredients in a screw-top jar and shake well to mix (alternately, whisk the ingredients together in a bowl).

3. Pour the dressing over the hot vegetables, toss and serve immediately.

aving finished his salad, Hugo let his gaze wander round the table. "Those, er, small cakes—what are they?"

Constance immediately served him one on a plate. "An ancient favourite from Brockhall. Actually, they're named after the place. Brockhall Badger Carrot Cakes, I've had the recipe with me since I was a tiny badgermaid. Would you like to hear it?"

Hugo bit into one and munched slowly. "Strange . . . I think I've tasted something like this before. Maybe I'm mistaken. Carry on. I'm curious to hear how they're made."

# BROCKHALL BADGER CARROT CAKES

*Serves 4*

## INGREDIENTS:

1 small potato, cooked and mashed (¾ cup)

3 medium carrots (6 ounces), peeled and grated

1 medium onion (6 ounces), peeled and grated

½ cup fresh breadcrumbs

2 teaspoons chopped fresh parsley

3 eggs, beaten

Salt and pepper, to taste

1 tablespoon vegetable oil

## METHOD:

1. Preheat the oven to 225° F. Place the potato in a bowl and mix in the carrot, onion, breadcrumbs and parsley.

2. Beat in the eggs and season well with salt and pepper.

3. Heat a little of the oil in a nonstick frying pan over medium heat and drop tablespoons of the batter into the pan. Cook until the undersides of the cakes are golden brown, turn them over and cook the other side, 3 to 4 minutes per side.

4. Transfer the cooked cakes to a paper towel-lined plate and keep warm in the oven. Continue with the remaining batter, adding oil to the pan as needed.

aving finished every crumb of the delicious cake, the Friar shook his head in puzzlement. "That's funny. It tasted just like the ones that I have made!"

Young Sister Pansy hastily pushed a small basin forward. "Friar Hugo, you must taste my Great Hall Gooseberry Fool. I invented it all by myself, and I named it, too."

Hugo smiled fondly at his young assistant. "I'll willingly try it, Pansy. I always knew you'd make a first-class cook since I first clapped eyes on you!"

Pansy blushed. "It's nice of you to say so, Friar. I must tell you the recipe— it'll sound a little bit like your method. But then, I learned all I know of cooking from the great Friar Hugo of Redwall."

# GREAT HALL GOOSEBERRY FOOL

## METHOD:

1. Place the gooseberries in a saucepan with the sugar and two tablespoons of water. Cook over medium heat until the fruit is completely soft, about 10 minutes. Press the fruit through a fine mesh sieve set over a bowl to achieve a smooth puree. Let cool.

2. To make the custard, in a bowl, mix the cornstarch and sugar with 2 tablespoons of the milk.

3. In a small saucepan over medium heat, bring the remaining ½ cup of milk to a boil. Pour the hot milk onto the cornstarch mixture and stir to blend well. Return the mixture to the pan and cook over medium-low heat, stirring, until thickened, about 4 minutes. Let cool, stirring occasionally.

4. Fold the custard and then the whipped cream into the gooseberry puree. Cover and refrigerate until thoroughly chilled, at least 1 hour.

5. To serve, divide the fool between four sundae glasses and sprinkle each with a little grated chocolate.

*Serves 4*

## INGREDIENTS:

### FRUIT:

1 pound gooseberries, washed

½ cup sugar

### CUSTARD   (or substitute ½ cup prepared vanilla pudding):

1 tablespoon sugar

1 tablespoon cornstarch

10 tablespoons milk

½ cup heavy cream, whipped

Grated chocolate (use a cheese grater), for serving

Friar Hugo had to stop himself from licking the small basin clean. "That was delightful, Sister Pansy. Thank you very much! Ah, Lady Cornflower, may I ask what was your offering to this Summer Orchard Picnic Tea?"

Cornflower bobbed a quick curtsy to the old Friar. "Cheerful Churchmouse Cherry Crisp! Would you like to try some, sir?"

Hugo chuckled. "Cheerful Churchmouse Cherry Crisp, eh? Sounds charming. Where did you learn to make it?"

Cornflower fidgeted with her apron. "Er—er—why, at Saint Ninian's old church. Mum used to make it after my dad had harvested his cherries. Eat up now, Friar, whilst I tell you how to make it."

# CHEERFUL CHURCHMOUSE CHERRY CRISP

*Serves 4*

## METHOD:

1. Preheat the oven to 400° F.

2. Place the cherries in a pie plate, sprinkle the sugar and 2 tablespoons of water over them, then bake until the cherries begin to soften, about 10 minutes.

3. Meanwhile, in a bowl, mix together the topping ingredients. Sprinkle this mixture over the cherries and return the dish to the oven until the topping is crisp and golden, 10 to 12 minutes.

## INGREDIENTS:

### FRUIT:

2 cups (12 ounces) fresh or frozen (thawed) cherries, stoned

1 ½ tablespoons sugar

### TOPPING:

¾ cup rolled oats

¼ cup Demerara (raw) sugar

¼ cup sliced almonds

2 tablespoons sesame seeds

4 teaspoons honey, warmed until runny

Hugo finished Cornflower's Cheerful Churchmouse Cherry Crisp. He picked a few crumbs from his whiskers and nibbled them. Licking his lips, he peered suspiciously at Cornflower. "Very nice, very nice indeed, marm. But it tastes awfully like my cherry crisp. Are you sure it was your mother's recipe you used?"

He did not notice that Lady Cornflower's paws were crossed behind her back as she answered.

"Oh, yes, Friar. She gave it the name because my dad used to say that it would keep any little Churchmouse cheerful."

Rosey Spike, who was Ambrose Spike's second cousin on his uncle's side, twice removed, nodded agreement with Cornflower. "Aye, 'tis right, Friar. I've eaten many a one meself, when I used to visit the Churchmouse family."

Friar Hugo smiled at the big, plump hedgehog. "I'll wager you have, marm. What's this you're giving me, eh? Not something made from another old family recipe, surely."

Rosey primped at the flowers set in her headspikes. "Certainly not, sir. These are me own personal recipe. I'm so proud of 'em that I named 'em meself. They're called Rosey's Jolly Raspberry Jelly Rock Cakes!"

Young Tummscoff broke out into a loud chortle. "Hawhawhaw! That's an absolute pip of a name, marm. Jolly Jelly Raspberry Rosey's Cake Rocks. Hawhawhaw! How's that for a blinkin' name, Nunky Baz, wot?"

Basil tweaked his cheeky nephew's ear. "Silly young rip. They're called Rockin' Rosey's Jelly Jolly Raspberry Cakes!"

Friar Hugo waved his dock leaf at the two hares. "Never mind what they're called. Let me sample one whilst Rosey tells me this new recipe she's so proud of!"

# ROSEY'S JOLLY RASPBERRY JELLY ROCK CAKES

*Makes 10 Rock Cakes*

## INGREDIENTS:

1 ¾ cups all-purpose flour, plus
    additional for rolling the dough

1 ½ teaspoons baking powder

½ teaspoon salt

6 tablespoons unsalted butter or
    margarine, chilled and cubed, plus
    additional for the baking sheet

½ cup sugar, plus additional for
    sprinkling

2 eggs, lightly beaten

Raspberry jam or jelly

## METHOD:

1. Preheat the oven to 400° F and grease a baking sheet.

2. In a mixing bowl, whisk together the flour, baking powder and salt. Add the butter and rub it into the flour with your fingers (alternately, pulse the dry ingredients and butter in a food processor) until the mixture resembles coarse crumbs. Stir in the sugar. Make a well in the centre, add the eggs and mix well to form a stiff dough.

3. Turn the dough out onto a floured board and form it into a roll. Cut the dough into ten pieces, shape them into balls and place them well apart on the baking sheet.

4. Use your thumb to make a hole in the centre of each and fill the hole with jam or jelly.

5. Pinch the dough closed over the jam, sprinkle the rock cakes with a little sugar and bake them until golden brown, about 15 minutes.

6. Cool the cakes on a wire rack and eat them while fresh, preferably on the same day.

After munching his way through one of the rock cakes, Hugo wiped his mouth on a napkin and mused, "Well now, Rosey Spike, if you hadn't told me that was your own recipe, I'd say it tasted like mine. "Hmm, er yes, what is it, my dears?"

Two little molemaids, Burrel and Roogul, were tugging at the Friar's wide sleeves. They curtsied and wrinkled their noses shyly, covering their faces with their flowery aprons. "You'm b'aint troid us'ns cooken yet, zurr."

Hugo's eyes lit up with pleasure at the molemaids' offering. "Ah, scones with strawberry jam and meadowcream. Thank the seasons for a good old-fashioned summer tea dish. I hope they haven't got a long tongue-twister of a name?"

Both molemaids chuckled and shuffled their footpaws. "Hurr hurr, nay, zurr. They'm jus' be called sconners wi' strawbee jam'n'gurt dollops o' ee meddycream."

Hugo carefully split one of the still-warm scones and spread it thickly with jam and cream. Taking a bite, he closed both eyes blissfully. "Now, that's what I call a proper traditional Redwall teatime treat. Well done, little missies. How did you make them?"

It took a bit of translating, but the good Friar listened intently as the molemaids mumbled on from behind their aprons.

# AFTERNOON TEA SCONES WITH STRAWBERRY JAM AND CREAM

*Makes 8 scones*

## INGREDIENTS:

1 ¾ cups all-purpose flour

2 teaspoons baking powder

1 teaspoon pumpkin pie spice (or a
   heaped ¼ teaspoon each ground
   cinnamon, ginger and nutmeg)

½ teaspoon salt

2 tablespoons unsalted butter, chilled
   and cubed

2 tablespoons sugar

⅔ cup skim milk

Strawberry jam and clotted cream
   (see Note) or whipped cream,
   for serving

## METHOD:

1. Preheat the oven to 450° F and place a baking sheet in
   it. In a mixing bowl, whisk together the flour, baking
   powder, pumpkin pie spice and salt.

2. Add the butter and rub it into the flour with your
   fingers (alternately, pulse the dry ingredients and
   butter in a food processor) until the mixture
   resembles coarse crumbs. Stir in the sugar.
   Add the milk and mix to form a soft dough.

3. Turn the dough out onto a floured work surface and
   use your hands to shape it into a thick 7-inch round.
   Cut the round into eight wedges.

4. Using oven mitts, carefully take the heated baking sheet out of the oven.
   With a spatula, transfer the scones to the baking sheet. Bake in the upper part
   of the oven until browned and well risen, 12 to 14 minutes.

5. Cool the scones on a wire rack and eat them while fresh, preferably on the same
   day. Serve with strawberry jam and cream.

## Note: CLOTTED CREAM

The traditional accompaniment to scones, jars of thick, rich, slightly tangy
clotted or Devonshire cream are sold in the refrigerator case of some gourmet
food shops. Whipped cream can be substituted, or try crème fraîche or whole
milk yogurt for a tangier option.

Hugo sat the two little molemaids beside him.

"Well, that was delicious, ladies. Thank you very much! Now, what will we try next? See anything you fancy?"

Roogul pointed a chubby paw at a big cake. "Mayn't uz troi ee gurt big un' o'er thurr, if et please ee?"

Hugo nodded his approval. "An excellent choice. I wonder who made it?"

Jess Squirrel, the mother of Noisy Sam, began slicing the cake for them as she explained. "This is my own Squirrelmum's Blackberry and Apple Cake. It's my Sam's favourite, but I'll serve you first."

Jess almost jumped at the sound of her son shouting.

"What ho, mum! Slice me off a big piece, too!"

She smiled fondly at Sam. "His appetite's as big as his voice, bless him. Now, two small slices for Burrel and Roogul, and a slightly larger one for you, Friar. Is there anything else I can get you?"

Hugo paused with a piece halfway to his mouth. "Just the recipe please, marm."

# Squirrelmum's Blackberry and Apple Cake

## Ingredients:

1 cup all-purpose flour

½ cup almond flour (or ½ cup sliced
   almonds, finely ground with
   a mortar and pestle)

6 tablespoons unsalted butter or
   margarine, softened, plus
   additional for the cake pan

6 tablespoons sugar

6 tablespoons apple juice

2 eggs

1 tablespoon baking powder

½ teaspoon salt

A few drops vanilla extract

1 cooking apple (such as Granny
   Smith), peeled, cored and
   chopped

1 cup fresh or frozen blackberries

1 tablespoon Demerara (raw) or
   granulated sugar, for sprinkling

## Method:

1. Preheat the oven to 400° F. Lightly grease an 8-inch
   cake pan (preferably springform) and line the bottom
   with parchment or waxed paper.

2. In a large bowl, beat together the flour, almond flour,
   butter, sugar, apple juice, eggs, baking powder, salt
   and vanilla extract.

3. Fold in the apple and blackberries and spoon the
   mixture into the cake pan. Sprinkle the Demerara
   sugar over the top and bake until golden and firm to
   the touch, 45 to 55 minutes.

4. Leave to cool on a wire rack (remove the sides of the
   pan if using a springform pan).

ugo moved his chair back a touch to gain a little shade as the sun moved westward in the sky. He patted his stomach. "Whew, I feel rather full. What a lovely afternoon tea. I must take a day off more often! Thank you, ladies."

An old shrewwife called Banka pushed a trolley to Hugo's side as he stifled a yawn. "Come on, sir. Don't you go droppin' off just yet. I'm sure you can manage a mouthful o' Guosim Shrew Shortbread an' a sip o' Strawberry Fizz?"

The old Friar blinked owlishly. "Wouldn't be summer tea without Strawberry Fizz, marm. Thankee. Guosim Shrew Shortbread, eh? I must try that. Great cooks, you Guosim." He took a small drop of the Strawberry Fizz. "Whoo! That's refreshing. Well done, Ambrose!"

Ambrose Spike, the Redwall Cellarhog, shook his head. " 'Tweren't I that made it, Friar, 'twas Sister Pansy. I'll give you her recipe later."

Hugo nibbled a shortbread. "Oh, wonderful! Nice soft taste, melts in the mouth. Tell me how you made it, Banka."

# GUOSIM SHREW SHORTBREAD

*Makes 16 wedges*

## INGREDIENTS:

2 ½ cups all-purpose flour

Pinch salt

1 cup (2 sticks) unsalted butter, chilled
   and cubed

½ cup sugar, preferably superfine,
   plus additional for sprinkling

## METHOD:

1. Preheat the oven to 325° F. Grease two 8-inch round cake pans and line the bottoms with parchment or waxed paper.

2. In a mixing bowl, stir together the flour and salt. Add the butter and rub it into the flour with your fingers (alternately, pulse the dry ingredients and butter in a food processor) until the mixture resembles coarse crumbs. Add the sugar and knead lightly to mix.

3. Press half the dough evenly into each pan. Bake until firm and golden, about 45 minutes.

4. Sprinkle sugar over the warm shortbreads and cut each round into eight wedges. Let cool in the pans.

oisy Sam was about to roar out for more cake when Constance placed a huge paw across his mouth.

"Hush, Sam, keep your voice down. Can't you see poor old Friar Hugo has dozed off?"

Good food, summer sun and the lazy afternoon had cast their spell. Hugo and the two little molemaids on either side of him had dropped off. Each of them still held a piece of shortbread in their paws.

Lady Cornflower fanned her brow and gave a soft sigh of relief. "Thank goodness for that! Do you think he suspected anything, Sister Pansy?"

The young mousemaid shook her head. "No, I think we kept him busy enough. Friar's so old that he hardly recognises one recipe from the other anymore. It's a good job he had them all noted down in his big kitchen book."

Lady Cornflower's husband, Matthias, looked from one lady to another in astonishment. "You don't mean to tell me they were all Hugo's own recipes you were using?"

Sister Pansy blushed furiously. "Yes sir, they were, but it wasn't using the recipes that bothered us. It was having to tell all those fibs to Friar Hugo."

Basil Stag Hare's usually floppy ears stood up rigid. "Wot, wot? Pretty ladies tellin' whoppin' great fibs? Well, singe m'whiskers! Don't you have enough recipes of your own?"

Constance nodded. "Aye, we've got recipes aplenty, but none like Friar Hugo's. That old mouse is Redwall's champion cook. Our recipes are quite good, but the Friar's are beyond compare. Isn't that right, Sister Pansy? Go on—tell him. 'Twas your idea after all."

Pansy explained to Matthias and Basil. "I could see that Friar needed a day off, so I thought up the plan. We'd make all the tea from Hugo's recipes and claim they were old family ones or that we'd invented them ourselves. There was no harm in it, sir. Look—he seems happy and peaceful enough."

Matthias chuckled. "Of course he does. It was a superb tea. Skipper, would you carry the Friar down to the gatehouse and put him in the big armchair there? It's cool and quiet. He won't be disturbed. So, come on, Sister Pansy. You still haven't told us how you made the great Strawberry Fizz."

Pansy giggled. "No more fibs, sir. Here's Friar Hugo's own recipe for Summer Strawberry Fizz."

Matthias looked puzzled. "I thought it was Ambrose Spike's. After all, he is the Chief Cellarhog of Redwall."

Ambrose quaffed a goblet of the fizz and winked. "I have to confess—I pinched the recipe from Hugo's book!"

Amid the stifled laughter, Skipper gently picked Hugo up as if he were a babe and carried him off to the gatehouse. Halfway across the lawn, Hugo opened one eye and whispered to the big, brawny otter.

"I hope Sister Pansy put my kitchen book back in its right place. I'd hate to lose it."

# SUMMER STRAWBERRY FIZZ

## METHOD:

1. Combine the strawberries, ice cream and sugar in a blender and process until smooth.

2. Refrigerate for one hour, then stir in the seltzer and serve immediately.

## INGREDIENTS:

1 quart (4 cups) strawberries, hulled

1 cup strawberry ice cream

4 teaspoons sugar

1 cup seltzer water

# Autumn

I saw the day dawn silent grey,
as sunrise mist turned gold.
Dame Autumn glided calmly in,
through summertime, grown old,
whilst apples ripe on orchard boughs
dropped to the wearied grass,
and dead leaves rustled to and fro
to let small breezes pass.
We harvested the oats and rye,
our barley and good wheat,
leaving birds, ere they flew south,
to glean all they could eat.
At harvest time, in autumntide,
dewy tears drip from the eaves,
sad legacy of summer days
are crimson, amber, russet leaves.

Mattimeo, son of Matthias and Cornflower, gathered his warm cloak about him and scanned the twilit orchard. Trees and bushes stood bare and forlorn, their fruits harvested by Redwallers, their dead leaves swept to the ground by autumnal breezes. The young mouse peered into the gathering gloom, his paws swishing through the leafy carpet as he paced to and fro. Mattimeo took his duties seriously; the Father Abbot had asked him to bring all the Dibbuns indoors.

Though his voice still squeaked a bit, Mattimeo tried to make it sound deeper as he called out sternly, "All Dibbuns indoors right away, please!"

There followed a chorus of infant giggles and a gruff molebabe's reply. "Us'ns b'aint yurr, zurr!"

Mattimeo could not help smiling to himself. He could recognise Bungo, the ringleader, anywhere.

"I know it's you, Bungo. Come on out and bring those other villains with you. Right now!"

Wind-drifted heaps of leaves rustled and shook with merriment as Bungo called back to him.

"Oi tole ee, Bungo bee's gonned, an' all ee likkle villyuns, too. Thurr bee's only uz leafs yurr!"

Mattimeo turned away from the quivering leaf heaps and shrugged as he strode from the orchard. "Well, I'm going inside. All you leaves can stay out here in the dark. That's the place for old dead leaves, out in the dark and cold for the night."

A little hogmaid's voice answered, trembling with dismay. "Some of us leafs wanna go back inside a h'Abbey!"

Mattimeo laughed and shook his head. "Oh, no. I'd only have to sweep 'em back out again. Good night, little leaves. I'll think of you when I'm down in Cavern Hole at the Autumn Harvest Homefeast. Poor leaves, out in the dark orchard, trying to hide from the Big Bad Bogey Beast!"

Mattimeo was suddenly knocked flat by a stampede of Dibbuns, shrieking and shouting as they fled from the orchard.

Down in Cavern Hole the lanterns glowed warmly around a huge buffet table, which was piled high with magnificent food. As if by magic, the Cavern suddenly filled with Abbeybabes, their eyes still wide with fright.

The Father Abbot chuckled as he sat down next to Cornflower. "Isn't it nice to see our Dibbuns right on time. Young Mattimeo has done a good job. There's not one of them missing."

Lady Cornflower clapped a paw to her mouth, stifling laughter at the sight of her son. Mattimeo looked slightly dazed as he was led in by Bungo. The molebabe brushed off some leaves clinging to the young mouse's cloak.

Bungo climbed up on Cornflower's lap and whispered solemnly to her, "Oi bringed yurr sunn 'ome, marm, ee felled over in ee leafs."

Cornflower stroked the tiny mole's velvety head. "That was a very kind thing to do. Thank you, Bungo."

The molebabe tugged his snout respectfully. "Moi pleasure, marm!"

The entire chamber fell silent as the Abbot said grace.

"Slumber long, you Autumn earth,
covered by your leaves, sleep on.
For the harvest that you gave,
we thank you, every one."

51

Everybeast applauded as Foremole started the proceedings by plunging his ladle into a large, steaming cauldron. Cornflower smiled at the look of joy on Bungo's face. "Do you like Deeper'n'Ever Turnip'n'Tater'n'Beetroot Pie, Bungo?"

The molebabe scrambled from her lap, doing a little dance of excitement. "Bo urr aye, marm! Thurr b'aint nuffin' loike et, speshully when ee Foremole bee's the cooker. Oi wunner as 'ow ee makes et?"

Cornflower winked secretly at the molebabe. "Why don't you go and ask him?"

A line of Redwallers had formed, all holding their bowls and basins to be filled. Foremole nodded affably to Bungo. "Ee cummed to 'elp oi, likkle zurr?"

Bungo tugged his snout and climbed up beside the mole leader. He began passing Foremole some bowls to fill. "Surrpintly, zurr, oi'll 'elp ee, if'n ee tells oi 'ow to be maken ee gurt deeper'n'ever pie."

Foremole chuckled. "That bee's a furr bargun, likkle 'un, but doan't ee fall into yon pot, or oi'll surve ee oop to summbeast. Yurr's 'ow ee makes et—lissun careful, naow!"

# MOLE'S FAVOURITE DEEPER'N'EVER TURNIP'N'TATER'N'BEETROOT PIE

*Serves 4*

## INGREDIENTS:

1 pound (3 medium) potatoes, peeled and chopped

Salt, to taste

$\frac{1}{2}$ pound (4 medium) carrots, peeled and chopped

$\frac{1}{2}$ pound turnips or rutabaga, peeled and chopped

6 tablespoons unsalted butter

Pepper, to taste

1 cup (2 ounces) grated Cheddar cheese (or any favourite hard cheese)

Crisp green salad, for serving (optional)

Pickled beets, for serving (optional)

## METHOD:

1. Preheat the oven to 350° F. Place the potatoes in a saucepan, cover with water and add a pinch of salt. Place the carrots and turnips or rutabaga in another saucepan, cover with water and add a pinch of salt. Boil all the vegetables until soft, 10 to 15 minutes.

2. Drain the vegetables separately, then return them to their pans and add half the butter to each pan. Mash the vegetables until they are smooth and season them with salt and pepper.

3. In a deep casserole dish, spread alternating layers of the mashed vegetables, starting with the carrot mixture and finishing with a layer of potato. Roughen the top with a fork.

4. Sprinkle the cheese on top and bake on the top shelf until the cheese is bubbling, about 15 minutes.

5. Serve with a crisp green salad and pickled beets if desired.

Ambrose Spike had his best barrel of October Ale on a trestle. He served Tim Churchmouse with a foaming beakerful.

"Drink hearty, Tim! Nothin' like good old October Ale to wet yore whistle. 'Tis the best I've brewed in many a season."

Tim took a long, slow sup. "Ah, that's the stuff to keep my paws strong for tolling the Redwall bells. I suppose it's a secret how you make it, eh, Ambrose?"

The Cellarhog hitched up his heavy apron. "Yore a good an' clever Bell-ringer, Tim, an' a fair cook by my reckonin'. Tell ye what—I'll do ye a trade. See that tasty lookin' dish you cooked? That'n on the table yonder?"

Tim eyed his creation proudly. "Aye, that's my special. Bellringer's Reward, I call it. Would you like me to fetch you a plate of it?"

Ambrose nodded. "I'd be pleased if ye did. Then if you tell me how y'made it, I'll give you my October Ale recipe. How does that sound to ye?"

Tim shook Ambrose's sturdy paw. "I'd call that a good offer!"

# BELLRINGER'S REWARD
## (ROAST ROOTS AND BAKED SPUDS)

## METHOD:

1. Preheat the oven to 375° F. Bring a large pot of water to a boil and salt it well. Add the vegetables and cook for 3 minutes, then drain.

2. Brush a rimmed baking sheet with some of the vegetable oil, add the vegetables, then drizzle the remaining oil over the vegetables and season with salt and pepper.

3. Bake until the vegetables are golden, about 30 minutes. Sprinkle with the parsley and serve.

## BAKED SPUDS:

## METHOD:

1. Preheat the oven to 400° F. Prick the potatoes all over with a fork. Place them in a roasting pan and drizzle with the olive oil. Sprinkle with salt, then shake the pan to coat the potatoes.

2. Bake for 90 minutes.

*Serves 4*

## INGREDIENTS:

## ROAST ROOTS:

Salt, to taste

1 small rutabaga (about 8 ounces), peeled and cut into 1-by-2-inch pieces

4 medium parsnips (about 8 ounces), peeled and cut into 1-by-2-inch pieces

4 medium carrots (about 8 ounces), peeled and cut into 1-by-2-inch pieces

2 tablespoons vegetable oil

Pepper, to taste

1 tablespoon finely chopped fresh parsley

## BAKED SPUDS:

4 large potatoes

2 teaspoons olive oil

Salt, to taste

Constance Badgermum and Sister Pansy watched Tim and Ambrose go sit on the stairs, where they ate and drank, whispering to one another between mouthfuls and swigs.

Pansy chuckled. "Look at those two, exchanging secret recipes."

Constance raised her eyebrows. "I'm surprised that Ambrose Spike would tell any of his recipes to another beast."

Pansy shrugged. "Fair exchange is no robbery, they say. Shall we move closer and listen in on them?"

Constance looked shocked at the suggestion. But she could not hide the mischievous twinkle in her eyes. "Yes, let's!"

Tim had finished imparting his recipe to Ambrose. The crafty Cellarhog glimpsed Constance and Pansy hovering close, so he winked at Tim and raised his voice a touch.

"First I gets a barrel o' muddy rainwater, then I soaks my apron in it for a day or two. Next I gets all the veggible peelings from Friar Hugo, the old moldy ones. Now you've got to stir 'em in with a few pawfuls of wild garlic . . ."

Constance and Pansy both pulled faces at each other and sidled off huffily. Ambrose waited until they were out of earshot. "Ho ho, that'll teach 'em to earwig on my recipes. Right, Tim mate, listen now—these are the real instructions."

# OCTOBER ALE

## METHOD:

Combine all the ingredients and serve chilled.

*Serves 2*

## INGREDIENTS:

2 cups ginger beer or ginger ale

1 cup grape juice

1 teaspoon sugar (omit if using
   ginger ale)

asil Stag Hare and his nephew Tummscoff were demolishing a tray of crispy biscuits between them. Friar Hugo drifted over and sat by them. "I see that you're both enjoying my Autumn Oat Favourites."

Tummscoff nodded briefly, speaking as he continued eating. "*Mmmff,* jolly tasty, *grmmff grrunch,* just the stuff t'give the troops, eh, Nunky Baz?"

Basil tweaked his cheeky nephew's ear. "I'll feed you to the bloomin' troops if you call me that again, young bounder. But he's right, Friar. Your biscuits are eminently munchable, sah, even if I do say so meself, wot!"

Hugo was not one to mince words—he came right to the point. "And what, may I ask, did you contribute to our Autumn Harvest Homefeast this evening?"

Basil twitched his nose in the direction of Hugo's bowl. "Oh, nothin' really. Just that stuff you appear to be scoffin'.
Enjoyin' it are you,
old lad?"

Hugo was taken aback. "You made this delicious mixture of berries and nuts? Well, I am surprised!"

Tummscoff left off stuffing himself for a moment. "Don't know why, old chap. My Nunk . . . er, Uncle Basil, sah, is a pretty good grubslinger. He used to make this when he was an Officer Cook with the sixty-seventh Paw an' Mouth Long Patrol. Calls it Hare's Haversack Crumble!"

Hugo shook his head in amazement. "Hare's Haversack Crumble?"

Basil looked dreamy as he recalled his old regimental days. "Ah, yes, old chap. Used to call it that because it came to bits in the haversacks, us bein' on the march all day. We used to pinch it out of one another's haversacks, y'know. Old Colonel Puffscutt always said it tasted better like that."

Hugo gave the hare a crafty wink. "No chance I could pinch the recipe from you, is there?"

Basil gestured over toward Ambrose and Tim. "I'll swap recipes with you, old scout. Seems to be the done thing at this feast, eh, wot?"

Hugo gnawed on his lip. He was not fond of giving away his Friar's secrets. Basil grinned roguishly at him.

"You pinch my recipe, an' I'll pinch yours. Honour among blinkin' pinchers. Shake?"

Hugo paused a moment, then stuck out his paw. "Shake!"

# AUTUMN OAT FAVOURITES

*Makes about 24 cookies*

## INGREDIENTS:

½ cup (1 stick) unsalted butter, plus additional for the baking sheets

½ packed cup light brown sugar

2 tablespoons golden syrup or corn syrup

¾ cup quick-cooking oats

¾ cup all-purpose flour

½ cup unsweetened grated coconut

1 teaspoon baking soda

## METHOD:

1. Preheat the oven to 325° F. Grease two baking sheets. Place the butter, sugar and syrup in a large saucepan. Heat gently until the butter has melted and the sugar has dissolved.

2. In a bowl, stir together the oats, flour and coconut, then stir this into the melted butter mixture.

3. In a small bowl, combine the baking soda with 1 teaspoon of hot water, then stir this mixture into the oat mixture.

4. When the dough is cool enough to handle, scoop up a tablespoon at a time, form it into a ball and place it on the baking sheet. Space the cookies at least two inches apart.

5. Bake until brown and crisp at the edges, 14 to 15 minutes.

# HARE'S HAVERSACK CRUMBLE

## INGREDIENTS:

### FRUIT:

1 quart (4 cups) fresh or frozen
   (thawed) blueberries or
   blackberries

2 tablespoons sugar, or to taste

### TOPPING:

1 cup all-purpose flour

6 tablespoons unsalted butter, at room
   temperature, cubed

1 teaspoon ground cinnamon

$\frac{1}{2}$ teaspoon salt

$\frac{1}{2}$ packed cup light brown sugar

$\frac{3}{4}$ cup chopped hazelnuts, pecans or
   any favourite nut

Custard sauce (see recipe, page 15) or
   ice cream, for serving

## METHOD:

1. Preheat the oven to 375° F. Place the berries in a large glass pie plate and sprinkle them with the sugar, adding a little more if the berries are very tart.

2. In a bowl, stir together the flour, cinnamon and salt. Add the butter and rub it into the flour with your fingers (alternately, pulse the dry ingredients and butter in a food processor) until the mixture resembles coarse crumbs. Mix in the brown sugar.

3. Sprinkle the crumble mixture evenly over the berries, then scatter the nuts over the top.

4. Bake until the topping is crisp and golden, 25 to 30 minutes.

5. Serve warm, with custard sauce or ice cream.

osey Spike, finding Matthias in a quiet corner, sat down by him, twiddling her spikes. Matthias smiled at her. "Something I can do for you, marm?"

Rosey sighed. "Look at 'em all, chatterin' away an' swapping favourite recipes. Nobeast's asked to exchange recipes with me, though."

Always gallant, Matthias patted his friend's paw. "Well, now, if you like my nutbread—Loamhedge Legacy, I call it—I'll trade recipes with you!"

Rosey agreed willingly. "Ooh, I love any sort of nutbread. Which one is yours?"

Matthias pointed. "Over there, by that big marvellous pudding. It's nothing so grand, I fear. Just a homely thing, but it's very tasty, and made to a real ancient recipe. Now, what's your offering for our feast, Rosey? Point it out."

Rather shyly, the hedgehog nodded toward the grand pudding that Matthias had been admiring. "That's it—my Harvestberry Sunset Pudd."

Matthias was astounded. "Great seasons, it's my lucky day. I'd give anything to be able to make a pudding like that!"

Rosey shook his paw heartily. "An' I'd love to know how to make your Loamhedge Legacy Nutbread. Aren't we both lucky? I'll go first!"

# HARVESTBERRY SUNSET PUDD

## METHOD:

1. In a saucepan over medium heat, combine the berries and honey. Bring to a simmer and cook for 10 minutes.

2. Line a deep round bowl with the bread, leaving no gaps. Spoon the cooked fruit into the bowl and top with the remaining bread, covering the fruit completely. Weigh down the pudding with a plate slightly smaller than the mouth of the bowl, and place something heavy (such as a can of beans) on top of the plate.

3. Refrigerate for 24 hours.

4. Gently unmold the pudding onto a serving plate and serve with lots of cream.

*Serves 6*

## INGREDIENTS:

1 pint (2 cups) fresh or frozen raspberries

1 pint (2 cups) fresh or frozen blackberries

6 tablespoons honey

One small loaf sliced white or wheat bread, crusts cut off

Whipped cream, for serving


# LOAMHEDGE LEGACY NUTBREAD

## METHOD:

1. Preheat the oven to 425° F. In a bowl, stir together the flour, baking powder, salt and cayenne pepper. Add the butter and rub it into the flour with your fingers (alternately, pulse the dry ingredients and butter in a food processor) until the mixture resembles coarse crumbs.

2. Stir in the milk and ⅔ cup of the pecans. Knead lightly to form a dough.

3. Turn the dough onto an ungreased baking sheet and pat it lightly into an eight-inch square. Use a knife to mark the dough into sixteen squares, cutting only partway down. Press the remaining ⅓ cup of nuts firmly into the top of the dough.

4. Bake until firm and golden, 22 to 24 minutes. Let cool for a few minutes, then break into squares and serve.

*Makes 16 squares*

## INGREDIENTS:

2 cups all-purpose flour

2 teaspoons baking powder

1 ½ teaspoons salt

¼ teaspoon cayenne pepper, or to taste

¼ cup (½ stick) unsalted butter, cubed

⅔ cup milk

1 cup chopped pecans

The feast almost finished, Redwallers sat back contented, patting their stomachs and loosening belts. Durdlum, one of Friar Hugo's kitchen assistants, accompanied by little Bungo, began distributing small dock leaf parcels from a trolley. Both he and Bungo were singing as they passed their delicacies out to one and all.

"Marms an' zurrs, moles an' hurrs,
do 'elp ee selfs to summ,
this'n yurr was maked by uz,
'tis vurry gudd, boi gumm!
Summthin' munchy, crunchy scrunchy,
in they'm parcels be,
summ furr all, an' summ furr thee,
an' summ furr ee an' me!"

The Father Abbot opened his parcel and sampled its contents. "Absolutely delicious! Who made this? What is it called?"

Durdlum tugged his snout respectfully. "Me'n Bungo maked em, zurr. They'm called Dibbun's Deloight!"

The Abbot munched some more. "Dibbun's Delight? You should call them Abbot's Delight. I must have the recipe!"

Baby Bungo shook his head solemnly. "Nay, zurr h'Abbot—us'ns b'aint given ee secret away. 'Tis far too vallybull!"

Cornflower came to the Abbot's assistance. "What a shame that Bungo and Durdlum won't give us their Dibbun's Delight recipe. Still, I know how hard it is to part with a secret like that. We wouldn't part with our secret recipe for Golden Hill Pears, would we, Father?"

The Abbot shook his head. "Oh, dearie me, no!"

At the mention of Golden Hill Pears, which was Bungo and Durdlum's favourite dessert, both moles cried out, "We'll swop ee recipe with ee!"

The Abbot tapped his paws thoughtfully on the table for quite a long time before giving his answer. "Oh, well . . . alright. You pair of young rogues!"

Bungo grinned from ear to ear. "Thankee, zurr, we'm bee's only young rogues, but one day when us'ns growed oop, we'll be ole rogues, loike ee!"

Mattimeo winked at Bungo. "Better than being a leaf out in the orchard, eh, Bungo?"

The little mole tucked into the last helping of Golden Hill Pears left on the feasting table. "Hurr, ennythin' bee's better'n that, zurr. Ho aye, zurr!"

# DIBBUN'S DELIGHT

*Makes about 4 dozen bars*

## INGREDIENTS:

3 cups (12 ounces) chopped mixed
    nuts

2 cups sugar

¾ cup light brown sugar

6 tablespoons golden syrup or corn
    syrup

¼ cup (½ stick) unsalted butter,
    plus additional for the pan

¼ teaspoon baking soda

## METHOD:

1. Preheat the oven to 225° F. Butter a 9-by-13-inch baking pan thoroughly. Place the nuts on a rimmed baking sheet and warm them in the oven until ready to use.

2. In a heavy saucepan over medium heat, combine the sugars, syrup, and 10 tablespoons (5 ounces) water and cook, stirring until the sugar dissolves.

3. Add the butter to the pan and bring the mixture to a boil. Simmer slowly, without stirring, until the liquid reaches 300° F (hard crack stage) on a candy thermometer, 20 to 25 minutes.

4. Quickly stir in the baking soda and the warmed nuts, and immediately pour the mixture into the greased pan.

5. Let cool until beginning to set (about 20 minutes), then use a sharp knife to mark approximately 1-by-2-inch bars. When completely cool, turn out of the pan and break into bars.

# GOLDEN HILL PEARS

## METHOD:

1. Put the sugar in the bottom of a heavy saucepan and sprinkle 2 tablespoons of water over it. Cook over medium heat without stirring until the mixture reaches a golden brown caramel, about 7 minutes. (Swirl the pan if the caramel colors unevenly).

2. Standing back, pour in $\frac{1}{4}$ cup of water, taking care as it will spit.

3. Add the pears and allspice to the pan, cover and simmer until the pears are tender, 10 to 15 minutes.

4. Use a slotted spoon to transfer the pears to a serving dish. Raise the heat and boil the syrup vigourously for 1 minute.

5. Pour the syrup over the pears and serve immediately, or let cool and then chill before serving.

*Serves 4*

## INGREDIENTS:

3 tablespoons sugar

4 medium pears, peeled, halved
  lengthwise and cored

Generous pinch ground allspice

# Winter

Hey ho, hey ho, now comes the snow,
as in draws early night,
outside the cold day slips away,
indoors the logs burn bright.
Long icicles hang from the trees,
like winter's daggers drawn,
whilst winds sing cruel dirges to
sad fields of stubble shorn.
Hear that rattling windowpane,
wriggle, snuggle, in your bed,
watch the pictures embers make,
pull the covers o'er your head.
We've food aplenty, warmth for all,
so let winter's snows preside.
Outside each day we'll sport and play,
and then at twilight, haste inside.

Young Sister Pansy was in such a state of excitement that she could hardly concentrate on her kitchen duties. Friar Hugo chuckled to Constance Badgermum as they watched her from across the kitchen.

"Our Pansy will burst with anticipation if the Abbey Wintersnow Ball doesn't start soon. Look, she can't stop her footpaws tapping!"

Suddenly, Pansy seized a broom and began dancing with it. Hugo put on a mock stern face as he called to her, "Sister Pansy, what in the name of seasons are you up to?"

The young mouse dropped the broom and came over to Hugo. "I'm sorry, Friar. I was just practising my waltz. I'm not too sure of how it goes. Can you show me, Constance, please?"

The big badger smiled. "What d'you think, Friar—shall I show her the right steps?"

Still with a stern face, hoping that Pansy would not see the twinkle in his eye, Hugo replied, "Work first, dance later, miss. This is the first time I've let you prepare a feast without my help, Pansy. Now tell me, have you done everything correctly?"

"Oh, yes, Friar. I helped all the duty workers to chop and peel, cooked it all by myself, helped to lay the trays out and dismissed the duty workers to go and get ready for the Ball. But how will I know when the dance starts if I'm out here in the kitchens?"

Constance spoke reassuringly. "Don't worry, Pansy. You'll hear the bells toll four times. That means Skipper and his crew are dragging the Winter Log in from Mossflower Wood. No need to fret, young 'un. There's a very special reason we've asked you to prepare the food by yourself. I'll tell you what we'll do. You take us around the kitchens and show us how you made each dish. If Friar Hugo is satisfied with your work, then I'll teach you how to dance properly. Agreed?"

Pansy bobbed a curtsy to Constance. "Oh, yes, please! Will you really teach me how to dance, and, er, what's the special reason why I had to prepare the food by myself?"

Friar Hugo folded both paws into his habit sleeves. "Just do as you're told, Sister Pansy, and stop asking questions. Right—show us the soup."

Pansy lifted the lid on the huge soup cauldron, reciting what she had learned from the Friar. "My first course is Shrimp'n'Hotroot Soup. There must be no shortage of this, as it's a great favourite with otters. They've been known to eat many basins of it at one sitting. This is how I went about making it."

# Shrimp'n'Hotroot Soup

## Ingredients:

2 tablespoons unsalted butter

1 large onion, chopped

2 medium leeks, washed well and
   chopped

1 ½ cups vegetable stock (or 1 ½ cups
   water and ½ cube vegetable
   bouillon)

3 medium potatoes, peeled and
   chopped

1 teaspoon curry powder or chili
   powder, or to taste

Salt and pepper, to taste

8 ounces peeled, cooked shrimp or
   prawns, sliced if large

1 cup milk

## Method:

1. In a large pot over medium heat, melt the butter.
   Add the onion and leeks and cook, stirring,
   until soft, about 5 minutes (do not let
   the vegetables brown).

2. Add the vegetable stock, potatoes, curry or chili
   powder, and salt and pepper. Cover and simmer until the potatoes are very soft,
   15 to 20 minutes.

3. Add the shrimp and milk and gently heat. Serve with crusty bread.

**C**onstance tried a small sip from the ladle tip. She fanned both paws in front of her mouth, blinking hard. "Whooo! It's a mite hot for me, but I don't think any otter could complain. You know what they say?"

Pansy did. "Ye can't make 'otroot 'ot enough for an otter!"

Friar Hugo nodded approvingly. "Very good. Next dish, please."

Pansy showed them a flat tray with delicious aromas emanating from it. "A great winter favourite with Foremole and his crew. Veggible Molebake. They like to eat it warm, often with some pickled beetroot slices on the side. Here's how it's made to the special recipe of Foremole's ancestors."

# VEGGIBLE MOLEBAKE

## INGREDIENTS:

2 tablespoons unsalted butter, plus
    additional for the pan

2 tablespoons all-purpose flour

¾ cup heavy cream

¾ cup vegetable stock or milk

2 egg yolks

Salt and pepper, to taste

2 cups (8 ounces) cauliflower florets,
    cooked

4 medium carrots (8 ounces), sliced
    and cooked

2 cups (10 ounces) peas, cooked

4 tomatoes, hulled and sliced

2 cups (4 ounces) grated Cheddar
    cheese

## METHOD:

1. Preheat the oven to 400° F. Butter a casserole or 9-by-13-inch baking pan. In a saucepan over medium heat, melt the butter. Sprinkle in the flour and cook, stirring, for 1 minute.

2. Gradually stir the cream and stock or milk into the flour mixture. Reduce the heat to low and cook, stirring, for 10 minutes.

3. In a bowl, beat the egg yolks well. Gradually whisk a few tablespoons of the hot liquid into the yolks, then whisk the yolks back into the saucepan. Heat, stirring, until the mixture just begins to steam (do not let it boil). Take the pan off the heat and stir for another minute or two to cool. Season the sauce with salt and pepper.

4. Spread the cauliflower in the bottom of the buttered baking dish. Layer in the carrots and then the peas. Pour the sauce over the casserole, then layer the tomato slices on top. Season well with salt and pepper and sprinkle the grated cheese over the top.

5. Bake until the cheese is melted, about 10 minutes. Turn on the broiler and broil the casserole, watching carefully, until the cheese is browned, 2 to 3 minutes.

With lots of appreciative noises and head-nodding, Hugo and Constance sampled a tiny portion. The Friar congratulated Pansy. "Hmmm, very good, extremely tasty—"

He was interrupted by the voices of Basil and Tummscoff calling hopefully from the kitchen entrance.

"Anyone in there, wot wot?"

"I say, can we lend a jolly old paw with the scoff?"

Hugo whispered to Pansy, "Remember what I told you about hares?"

Pansy rolled up her sleeves and grabbed a big wooden ladle. She strode to the door, a grim look on her pretty face as she roared out in her gruffest voice, "Be off with you, y'great slab-sided, famine-faced, pot-bellied, flop-eared villains! Move yourselves before I flatten your bottle-nosed snouts with me ladle. Go on, be off!"

There was a shuffle of retreating paws and huffy remarks. "Huh, that's what a chap gets for offerin' his bally help. Insults an' the threat of a hard ladlin', wot?"

"Sounds like a blinkin' madbeast. Best make ourselves scarce, Nunky Baz, wot, wot? Yowch!"

"I'll Nunky Baz you, young rip. Mind y'manners, sah!"

Pansy returned, pale-faced and shaking. "I wasn't too hard on them, was I, Friar?"

Hugo winked at her. "No, Sister, you hit just the right note. Always remember, a hare in the kitchen is like a horde of vermin in a strawberry patch. Well done, miss. Now, what's next?"

Pansy lifted a pan lid with a flourish. "Stones inna Swamp!"

Hugo explained to Constance. "Parsley dumplings in bean soup. But the Dibbuns won't have it by any other name than Stones inna Swamp. Carry on with the recipe, Pansy."

# STONES INNA SWAMP

## INGREDIENTS:

### BEAN SOUP:

1/2 cup dried white beans

1/2 cup dried kidney beans

4 teaspoons vegetable oil

1 1/2 cups (1 large) sliced onion

2 celery stalks, chopped

1 garlic clove, crushed

1 1/2 cups (4 ounces) sliced mushrooms

2 green bell peppers, seeded and
    chopped

1 cup vegetable stock (or 1 cup water
    and 1/2 cube vegetable bouillon)

1 can (14 ounces) chopped tomatoes

1 tablespoon chopped parsley

1 teaspoon paprika

Salt and pepper, to taste

### PARSLEY DUMPLINGS:

1 cup rolled oats

1/2 cup breadcrumbs (preferably
    whole wheat)

2 teaspoons chopped parsley

1/4 cup margarine

1/2 cup grated Cheddar cheese

## METHOD:

1. To make the soup, soak the dried beans in water overnight.

2. Drain the soaked beans and transfer them to a large pot. Add water to cover and bring to a boil. Boil the beans for 15 minutes, then reduce the heat and simmer until the beans are completely cooked, 40 to 50 minutes more. Drain.

3. In a large, preferably nonstick frying pan over medium heat, warm the oil. Add the onion, celery and garlic and cook, stirring, for 5 minutes. Add the mushrooms and peppers and cook, stirring occasionally, for 3 more minutes.

4. Add the beans, stock, tomatoes, parsley and paprika. Season with salt and pepper.

5. Bring to a boil, cover partially, and simmer for 20 minutes, stirring occasionally.

6. To make the dumplings, stir together the oats, breadcrumbs, parsley and salt in a bowl. Add the margarine and rub it into the dry ingredients with your fingers until evenly distributed. Stir in 2 to 3 tablespoons of cold water, until the mixture just forms a dough.

7. Form the dough into twelve 1 ½-inch round dumplings. Add the dumplings to the bean mixture and reduce the heat to low. Simmer, covered, turning the dumplings after 10 minutes, until they are cooked through, another 20 to 25 minutes.

8. Sprinkle with the grated cheese and serve.

Constance licked her apron dreamily. "A favourite from my young days, though we called it Boulders inna Marsh. Strange how Dibbuns like food to have dreadful-sounding names. D'you remember Fried Frogs an' Rickyroots?"

Hugo clapped a paw to his brow. "Don't remind me!"

Pansy giggled. "What were Fried Frogs an' Rickyroots?"

Constance shook her head. "I won't even begin to tell you. Ooh, this looks nice, Pansy. What is it?"

Pansy beamed proudly. "Savoury Squirrel Bakes. The recipe goes right back to a Squirrel Queen called Lady Amber."

Friar Hugo cut two tiny slices. "I see you've done your research, too. That's important, Pansy. We must never forget where and how good food was made, and who first made it. Mm, couldn't have baked better myself. Tell Constance how you produced it, please."

# SAVOURY SQUIRREL BAKES

*Serves 4*

## INGREDIENTS:

1 pound potatoes, boiled and mashed

2 cups (4 ounces) grated hard cheese,
   such as Cheddar

2 tablespoons unsalted butter, softened

1 tablespoon chopped chives or
   scallions

Salt and pepper, to taste

1 to 2 tablespoons all-purpose flour,
   as needed

1 egg, beaten

1 cup breadcrumbs

## METHOD:

1. Preheat the oven to 375° F. In a bowl, beat the potatoes with the cheese, butter, chives, salt and pepper until smooth. If the dough is too loose to handle, stir in enough flour, up to 2 tablespoons, to make a firm dough.

2. Turn the dough onto a floured board and form it into a 2-inch-thick log. Cut the dough into 1-inch slices and shape the slices into balls.

3. Set up a bowl with the egg in it and a bowl with the breadcrumbs. Coat each ball of dough in egg, then breadcrumbs, then place it on a baking sheet. Bake until browned, about 20 minutes (alternately, fry the cakes over medium heat in about $\frac{1}{4}$ inch of vegetable oil until browned on all sides, about 5 minutes).

Constance took a second slice. "We'd best not put all this on display in Great Hall, or nobeast will dance once they see it."

Pansy tugged at the badger's apron. "About the dancing, marm—are you sure you can teach me in such a short time?"

Constance tweaked the mousemaid's ear playfully. "Let me worry about that. What have you got to show us next?"

Pansy halted by a trolley draped in a tablecloth. "It's a good job Basil and Tummscoff never saw this. Look!"

She swept the cloth off, appreciating the small gasps of admiration from her seniors. Friar Hugo circled the trolley, murmuring to himself, "You've excelled yourself, Pansy!"

Pansy lowered her eyes, blushing. "You'll be making me swell-headed with compliments like that, Friar."

Constance let her eyes wander over the sweet-looking dish. "Huh, I'd be swell-headed, too, if I could make something like this. How did you manage it, you young genius?"

Friar Hugo tapped Constance's paw lightly as she reached out. "Don't touch, marm. 'Twould be a shame to spoil such a masterpiece. Right, ask her the riddle, Pansy."

The young mousemaid smiled at the friar, before asking the others, "What has the stone on the inside and the stone on the outside?"

Constance shook her head. "I'd never guess in a hundred seasons. You'll have to tell me."

Pansy explained, "This is really a plum and almond thing. The plum has its stone on the inside, but the almond has a stone around the outside of it. So Friar Hugo and I called this Outside'n'Inside Cobbler Riddle. I'll tell you how it's made."

# OUTSIDE 'N' INSIDE
# COBBLER RIDDLE

*Serves 8*

## INGREDIENTS:

## FRUIT:

3 to 4 pounds mixed fruits, such as
    peaches, plums, nectarines and
    apricots, pitted and roughly
    chopped (10 cups)

6 tablespoons light brown sugar

3 tablespoons all-purpose flour

Grated zest of 1 small orange

## METHOD:

1. Preheat the oven to 375° F. Butter a 9-by-13-inch baking pan.

2. In a bowl, toss the fruit with the brown sugar, flour and orange zest (it's easiest to use your hands). Spread the fruit mixture in the baking pan.

3. For the topping, whisk together the flour, almond flour (or ground almonds), sugar, baking powder and salt. Add the egg, yogurt, butter and vanilla and stir gently until just combined.

4. Drop spoonfuls of the topping onto the fruit, leaving a 1-inch border of fruit all round the outside. Sprinkle the almonds on top.

5. Bake the cobbler until the topping is well browned and a toothpick inserted into the center comes out clean, 50 to 55 minutes.

6. Serve warm, dusted with confectioners' sugar, with whipped cream to accompany.

## TOPPING:

1 cup all-purpose flour

½ cup almond flour (or ½ cup sliced almonds, finely ground with a mortar and pestle)

½ cup sugar

2 ½ teaspoons baking powder

¼ teaspoon salt

1 egg

⅓ cup plain yogurt

6 tablespoons unsalted butter, melted and cooled, plus additional for the pan

½ teaspoon vanilla extract

2 tablespoons sliced almonds

Confectioners' sugar and whipped cream, for serving

Constance sampled a morsel. "Strange name, but a lovely taste. Any more surprises with funny names, Pansy?"

The housemaid drew a basin from the oven. She offered some of its contents on a spoon. "Careful, it's quite hot!"

Constance blew on it and tasted gingerly. "Now, that's what I call a really good rhubarb pudding!"

Pansy placed it carefully back into the oven. "Well, you'd better not let baby Bungo hear you calling it that. I let him name it. D'you know what he called it?"

The badger shook her head. "Something awful, I'll be bound."

Pansy laughed. "No, no. Bungo calls it Rubbadeedubb Pudd. It's a jolly-sounding name. I like it!"

Constance licked her lips. "Tastes a lot better than it sounds. I'll feel silly asking somebeast to pass the Rubbadeedubb Pudd."

Friar Hugo fanned his face with the dock leaf on his tail. "Aye, so will I, but I'll swallow my pride and ask anyhow. Come on then, Sister. Give us the recipe."

# RUBBADEEDUBB PUDD

*Serves 6*

## INGREDIENTS:

¾ cup all-purpose flour

1 teaspoon baking powder

¼ teaspoon salt

¼ cup (½ stick) unsalted butter or
    margarine, cubed, plus additional
    for the pan

½ cup sugar, plus additional for serving

1 pound rhubarb, trimmed, cleaned,
    and cut into 1-inch slices

⅔ cup milk

## METHOD:

1. Preheat the oven to 400° F and butter a 9-by-13-inch baking pan.

2. In a mixing bowl, whisk together the flour, baking powder and salt. Add the butter or margarine and rub it into the flour with your fingers (alternately, pulse the dry ingredients and butter in a food processor) until the mixture resembles fine breadcrumbs.

3. Stir in the sugar and rhubarb and beat in the milk until incorporated. Scrape the batter into the baking dish and bake until the top is golden brown and a toothpick inserted into the center comes out clean, 35 to 45 minutes.

4. Serve immediately, with sugar for sprinkling.

C onstance looked around the trolleys. "Anything else the moles have thought up? I like molefood—it has a nice, homely taste to it."

Pansy picked up a dumpy-shaped little pastry. "Try a Nunnymoler."

Constance scratched her great striped muzzle. "A Nunny what?"

Friar Hugo broke the pastry in two and gave Constance half. "Molewives bake them for the little ones. They were supposed to be called Honey Moles, but in molespeak they're known as Nunnymolers. Tell her how you make them, Pansy."

# NUNNYMOLERS

*Makes 12*

## METHOD:

1. Preheat the oven to 350° F. In a bowl, whisk together the flour and confectioners' sugar. Add the butter or margarine and rub it into the flour with your fingers (alternately, pulse the dry ingredients and butter in a food processor) until the mixture resembles fine breadcrumbs. Sprinkle in 3 to 4 tablespoons ice water, mixing with a fork (or pulsing in the food processor) until a dough forms.

2. Divide the dough into twelve 2-inch balls. Use your palm or a rolling pin to flatten each ball into a 5-inch round.

3. Spread each round with a thin layer of honey. Place 1 strawberry and 1 raspberry in the middle of each piece of dough, then fold the edges of dough in toward the center, leaving a small opening in the middle, and pinch the folds of dough together. Put a dollop of jam into the top of each Nunnymoler.

4. Bake until firm and golden, 20 to 25 minutes. Let cool on a wire rack before serving.

## INGREDIENTS:

3 cups all-purpose flour

1/2 cup confectioners' sugar

1 cup (2 sticks) unsalted butter or
margarine, cubed

12 strawberries, hulled

12 raspberries

Honey

Raspberry or strawberry jam

he badger munched away happily. "Ha ha, then Nunnymolers it is!"

Hugo began untying his apron strings. "Is that the lot, Pansy?"

The mousemaid smiled secretly as she swung open the larder door. "Oh, no, Friar. This is a creation of my own. Applesnow!"

Hugo raised his eyebrows as he peered into the larder. "Applesnow, what a nice name. It looks delicious. Can I try it?"

Constance tugged the Friar gently back by his habit. "No, let's keep it as Pansy's surprise until the feast. Tell me, miss. Why didn't you call it Snow Apples?"

Pansy closed the larder door. "Because I think the name Applesnow has a nicer sound to it. You and Friar are the first ones to hear this recipe."

# APPLESNOW

*Serves 4*

## INGREDIENTS:

1 large sauce apple (such as McIntosh or Cortland), peeled, cored, and thinly sliced

1 teaspoon ground cinnamon (optional)

Sugar (or other sweetener), to taste

1 egg white (see Note)

## METHOD:

1. Place the apple slices in a saucepan with the cinnamon, if using, and add 2 tablespoons of water. Bring to a boil over medium heat, then cover the pan, reduce the heat, and simmer until the apple goes mushy, 5 to 10 minutes.

2. Transfer the apple mush to a bowl, add the sugar, and beat until smooth. Let cool.

3. Just before serving, beat the egg white in a mixer until stiff. Fold the egg white into the apple and serve.

## Note: RAW EGG WHITES

For most healthy people, the risk of salmonella food poisoning from a fresh egg white is small. To minimise this risk, use the egg white directly from the refrigerator and serve immediately, or, to avoid all risk, substitute powdered egg whites. Follow package directions to reconstitute the equivalent of one white.

ansy spread her paws wide and bowed. "So, there you have it—a nine-course banquet for the Ball!"

Friar Hugo stifled a smile. "This'll be the first Ball I've attended where there's nothing to drink!"

Pansy clapped a paw to her mouth. "Oops, sorry! I forgot the special Mossflower Mulled Cider!"

The Friar sniffed his way across the kitchen to a huge bowl. "I never forgot it. I could smell it from here. It's the one thing I remember from winter celebrations since I was a Dibbun, the most wonder-ful aroma!"

Pansy curtsied. "Thank you, Friar. Here's how I made it."

# MOSSFLOWER MULLED CIDER

## METHOD:

1. In a saucepan over medium heat, combine the cider, sugar, cloves, cinnamon and allspice and stir together until the sugar has dissolved. Continue to heat until the cider reaches a boil.

2. Take the pan off the heat, cover it, and let sit for 10 to 15 minutes. Strain out the whole spices and serve warm, garnished with a lime or lemon slice.

*Serves 2*

## INGREDIENTS:

2 cups apple cider

3 tablespoons sugar

4 cloves

1 cinnamon stick

Pinch ground allspice

2 slices lime or lemon

A voice sounded from the kitchen doorway. "Are you ready for me yet, Miz Constance?"

The badger called back, "Good timing. Come on in, Sprywisp!"

A young mouse entered, dashingly handsome, clad in a green velvet cape and wearing a round red cap with a lark feather in it. Sweeping off the cap, he bowed gallantly to Pansy. "At y'service, miss. I'm to be your dance teacher."

The mousemaid trembled as she returned a curtsy. "Sprywisp, the famous travelling dancer?"

His smile lit up the kitchen. "Invited specially to your Abbey Wintersnow Ball by Miz Constance. But not to dance with her. I'm to be your partner this evening."

Pansy was flustered. "But—but, I'm still in my working apron. I've not changed yet."

Sprywisp gestured at his garb. "And I'm still in my travelling clothes. What difference? It will be a great honour to dance with the Head Cook of Redwall Abbey."

Pansy pointed at herself. "Who, me? B-but I'm only Sister Pansy, the assistant to Friar Hugo."

Constance put a paw about Pansy. "No longer. That was why you were ordered to prepare all the food by yourself. Friar Hugo is going to retire. Oh, he will still be here to advise you, if need be. Pansy, you came through the test with flying colours. Henceforth, you are Head Cook of Redwall Abbey. Tonight at the Ball our Father Abbot will announce it."

Pansy would never forget that evening as long as she lived.

Dressed in a pale green and cream ribboned gown (which Cornflower had made for her), she was cheered to the rafters by Redwallers for the wonderful spread she had created for them. After the Father Abbot had confirmed to all Pansy's new position as Head Cook of Redwall, the music struck up. Squirrel fiddlers, otter drummers, mice on flutes, hedgehogs shaking tambourines. Pansy took her place, with Sprywisp, at the head of the dancers. She was radiantly confident, having already practised the waltz four times around the kitchen with the dancing master. A chorus of Abbeymaids sang the Ball Song in time to the musicians. Pansy felt as though her paws never touched the worn old sandstone floor. She glided around the Great Hall with Sprywisp, both of them joining in the song.

"Now we're all assembled here in Great Hall,
every creature in their best finery.
Winter's such a lovely time at Redwall,
would you like to take a dance, marm, with me?

So bow to your partner, sir,
hold your paws out wide,
twice round the floor here,
'tis the Abbey sleigh ride.

Though 'tis cold outside, we're all warm in here,
twirl your partner round the room gracefully.
Coloured lanterns glow with such cosy cheer,
at the feast tonight, will you sit with me?
Twiddle to the fiddle,
on the drumbeat skip aside,
join your paws in the middle,
'tis the Abbey sleigh ride!"

as there ever such an Abbey Wintersnow Ball? Were there ever such happy creatures gathered in one place? Such music, dancing and gaiety.

As for the food, even baby Bungo, when he was a fat old mole, could still recall it in dreams.

# INDEX

**DRINKS**

Hot Mint Tea, 21

Mossflower Mulled Cider, 89

October Ale, 57

Summer Strawberry Fizz, 45


**SOUPS / APPETISERS**

Hare's Pawspring Vegetable Soup, 5

Shrimp'n'Hotroot Soup, 73

Stones inna Swamp, 78

Stuffed Springtide Mushrooms, 13


**MAIN DISHES / SAVOURY SIDES**

Bellringer's Reward (Roast Roots and Baked Spuds), 55

Brockhall Badger Carrot Cakes, 32

Crispy Cheese'n'Onion Hogbake, 7

Gourmet Garrison Grilled Leeks, 11

Hotroot Sunsalad, 31

Mole's Favourite Deeper'n'Ever Turnip'n'Tater'n'Beetroot Pie, 53

Savoury Squirrel Bakes, 81

Vegetable Casserole à la Foremole, 9

Veggible Molebake, 75


**DESSERTS / AFTERNOON TREATS**

Abbot's Special Abbey Trifle, 15

Afternoon Tea Scones with Strawberry Jam and Cream, 39

Applesnow, 88

Autumn Oat Favourites, 60

Cheerful Churchmouse Cherry Crisp, 35

Custard Sauce, 15

Dibbun's Delight, 66

Golden Hill Pears, 67

Great Hall Gooseberry Fool, 33

Guosim Shrew Shortbread, 42

Hare's Haversack Crumble, 61

Harvestberry Sunset Pudd, 63

Honeybaked Apples, 19

Loamhedge Legacy Nutbread, 63

Nunnymolers, 87

Outside'n'Inside Cobbler Riddle, 84

Rosey's Jolly Raspberry Jelly Rock Cakes, 37

Rubbadeedubb Pudd, 86

Spiced Gatehouse Tea Bread, 17

Squirrelmum's Blackberry and Apple Cake, 41